(Early Intermediate)

Cool Classics
Level Three

For Piano Solo
Compiled and Arranged by Wesley Schaum

Forword

This book offers a unique approach to classics for the piano student. Familiar themes by classic composers are presented in two, and sometimes three sections forming a medley. In the first section, the theme is arranged in traditional style. The second and third sections are written in contrasting and embellished versions. Many of the embellishments are lighthearted caricatures with syncopations in a jazzy style. Others are enhanced with contemporary harmonies, imaginative bass lines and counter melodies.

Students will enjoy the stylistic changes and subtle humor that makes these pieces fun to play and terrific for recitals. This series consists of three books, Level 2, Level 3 and Level 4.

Index

Title	Composer	Page
Air in C (from "Marriage of Figaro")	Mozart	10
Brother Come and Dance With Me (from "Hansel and Gretel")	Humperdinck	13
Dance of the Sugar Plum Fairy (from "The Nutcracker")	Tchaikowsky	8
Flowers That Bloom In the Spring (from "The Mikado")	Sullivan	16
Hallelujah Chorus (from "The Messiah")	Handel	22
Melody (from "Album for the Young")	Schumann	4
My Heart Ever Faithful (from Cantata, BWV 68)	Bach	20
Toreador March (from "Carmen")	Bizet	6
Waltz (Op. 39, No.15)	Brahms	18
William Tell March	Rossini	2

Schaum Publications, Inc. • 10235 N. Port Washington Rd. • Mequon, WI 53092
www.schaumpiano.net

© Copyright 2010 by Schaum Publications, Inc., Mequon, Wisconsin
International Copyright Secured • All Rights Reserved • Printed in U.S.A.
ISBN-13: 978-1-936098-23-1

Warning: The reproduction of any part of this publication without prior written consent of Schaum Publications, Inc. is prohibited by U.S. Copyright Law and subject to penalty. This prohibition includes all forms of printed media (including any form of photocopy), all forms of electronic media (including computer images), all forms of film media (including filmstrips, transparencies, slides and movies), all forms of sound recordings (including cassette tapes and compact disks), and all forms of video media (including video tapes and DVD).

William Tell March

Gioacchino Rossini (1792-1868)

Melody
(from "Album for the Young")

Toreador March
(from "Carmen")

Moderato ♩ = 100-108

George Bizet (1838-1875)

Dance of the Sugar Plum Fairy

(from "The Nutcracker")

Peter I. Tchaikowsky (1840-1893)

Air in C
(from "Marriage of Figaro")

Wolfgang Amadeus Mozart (1756-1791)

Brother Come and Dance With Me

(from "Hansel and Gretel")

Engelbert Humperdinck (1854-1921)

Flowers That Bloom In the Spring
(from "The Mikado")

Sir Arthur Sullivan (1842-1900)

Waltz
(Op.39, No.15)

Johannes Brahms (1833-1897)

My Heart Ever Faithful

(from Cantata, BWV 68)

Johann Sebastian Bach (1685-1750)

Hallelujah Chorus
(from "The Messiah")

George Frederick Handel (1685-1759)